WARNING!

THESE JOKES WILL ANNOY EVERYONE YOU KNOW

WARNING!

THESE JOKES WILL ANNOY EVERYONE YOU KNOW

PENGUIN BOOKS

CONTENTS

TOO (UN)COOL FOR SCHOOL

What do kids do during recess on rainy days?

Play bored games.

Why did the student eat his homework?

The teacher told him it was a piece of cake.

What do elves learn in school?

The elf-abet.

Why was the broom late to class?

It over-swept.

What is a snake's favourite subject?

Hisssssstory.

Why did the teacher wear sunglasses to school?

Her students were so bright.

What time would it be if Godzilla came to school?

Time to run.

Why did the dog get straight As in school?

He was the teacher's pet.

Why did the kids cross the playground?

To get to the other slide.

Why do magicians do well in school?

They are very good at trick questions.

What kind of school do surfers attend?

Boarding school.

What should you do if a teacher rolls her eyes at you?

Pick them up and roll them back.

Why did the jelly bean go to school?

To become a smartie.

Why are fish so smart?

They live in schools.

What did the paper say to the pencil?

'Write on!'

Which contest does a skunk always win at school?

A smelling bee.

Why do music teachers need ladders?

To reach the high notes.

Why did the square and the triangle go to the gym?

To stay in shape.

Which animal cheats on exams?

The CHEAT-ah.

Did you hear about the cross-eyed teacher?

He couldn't control his pupils.

Why did the student steal a chair from the classroom?

The teacher told him to take a seat.

When is a blue school book not a blue school book?

When it is read.

What did one calculator say to the other?

'You can count on me.'

How did the music teacher get locked out of her classroom?

Her keys were on the piano.

What did the glue say to the teacher?

'I'm stuck on you.'

Why did the bat miss the school bus?

It hung around for too long.

How do you get straight As?

Use a ruler.

If you had six apples, three oranges, five strawberries and two blueberries, what would you get?

A fruit salad.

Why is 2+2=5 like your left foot?

It's not right.

Why did the teacher go to the beach?

To test the water.

Five frantic frogs fled from fifty fierce fishes.
She sells seashells by the seashore.

Peter Piper picked a peck
of pickled peppers
A peck of pickled peppers
Peter Piper picked
If Peter Piper picked a peck
of pickled peppers
Where's the peck of pickled
peppers Peter Piper picked?

MUSICAL MAYHEM

What musical instrument is found in the bathroom?

A tuba toothpaste.

How does the sun listen to music?

On its ray-dio.

What is Beethoven doing now?

De-composing.

What makes music in your hair?

A head band.

What happens when you hear music coming from the printer?

The paper is jamming.

How do you make a bandstand?

Take away all the chairs.

What is a golf club's favourite kind of music?

Swing.

What do you call a cow who plays a musical instrument?

A moo-sician.

What do you get when you put a radio in the fridge?

Cool music.

Which band musician performs with the most force?

Oboe-Wan Kenobi.

What is a cat's favourite song?

'Three Blind Mice'

Why did the grandma sit in her rocking chair wearing rollerblades?

She wanted to rock-and-roll.

What has forty feet and sings?

The school choir.

What is a pirate's favourite instrument?

A guitarrrrrr.

What kind of music do balloons hate?

Pop music.

What part of a fish is the most musical?

Its scales.

Why couldn't the athlete listen to her music?

She broke the record.

How does a witch play loud music?

On her broom box.

Why did the pianist keep banging her head against the piano keys?

She was playing by ear.

What song do vampires hate?

'You Are My Sunshine'

What's the difference between a recorder and an onion?

Nobody cries when you chop up a recorder.

What is a frog's favourite kind of music?

Hip hop.

What did the musical director do when the cellist cut his finger?

Gave him a band-aid.

Which band musician wears the biggest sneakers?

The one with the biggest feet.

Why does a concert hall get warm after a band plays?

All the fans have left.

Why is a piano so hard to open?

The keys are on the inside.

What's green and sings?

Elvis Parsley.

What is a windmill's favourite kind of music?

Heavy metal.

Which Star Wars character never liked playing along with the other musicians?

Han Solo.

Why are pirates good singers?

They can hit the high Cs.

CHRISTMAS CRACK-UPS

What do you call a reindeer with bad manners?

Rude-olph.

What happened to the man who stole an Advent calendar?

He got 25 days.

What do you get when Santa becomes a detective?

Santa Clues.

How can you help someone who has lost their Christmas spirit?

Nurse them back to elf.

Why did the scarecrow get a big Christmas bonus?

He was outstanding in his field.

What did the bald man say when he got a comb for Christmas?

'I'll never part with it.'

What is a vegan's favourite Christmas carol?

'Soy to the World'

How does a snow globe feel at Christmas?

A little shaken.

What was Santa's favourite subject in school?

Chemis-tree.

What is the name of Santa's dog?

Santa Paws.

What happens when Christmas elves are cheeky?

Santa gives them the sack.

What kind of photos do elves take?

Elfies.

What does Santa suffer from if he gets stuck in a chimney?

Claus-trophobia.

Who hides in the bakery at Christmas?

A mince spy.

What did the Christmas tree do after its bank closed?

It started its own branch.

How does Darth Vader enjoy his Christmas turkey?

On the dark side.

What do they sing at a snowman's birthday party?

'Freeze a Jolly Good Fellow!'

How do Christmas trees get their email?

They log on.

Why did Santa's helper see the doctor?

He had low elf-esteem.

What do you get if you cross Santa with a duck?

A Christmas quacker.

What do you call Santa when he stops moving?

Santa Pause.

What is the best Christmas present in the world?

A broken drum – you just can't beat it.

Why did the Christmas tree go to the dentist?

It needed a root canal.

Who delivers presents to baby sharks at Christmas?

Santa Jaws.

Why are Christmas trees so bad at sewing?

They always drop their needles.

How do snowmen get around?

They ride an icicle.

Which carol is heard in the desert?

'O Camel Ye Faithful'

What do you get if you eat Christmas decorations?

Tinsilitis.

What's green, covered in tinsel and goes *ribbet ribbet*?

Mistle-toad.

What did the stamp say to the Christmas card?

'Stick with me and we'll go places.'

Why is it getting harder to buy Advent calendars?

Their days are numbered.

Which of Santa's friends is the most chill?

Jack Frost.

Why don't crabs celebrate Christmas?

Because they're shell-fish.

What do you call a reindeer who can't see?

No-eye deer.

What is a parent's favourite Christmas carol?

'Silent Night'

Which of Santa's reindeers has the best moves?

Dancer.

What does Santa spend his money on?

Jingle bills.

What was the snowman doing in the vegetable patch?

Picking his nose.

How do sheep greet each other at Christmas?

'Merry Christmas to ewe!'

How do you turn a Christmas tree into a reindeer?

You decorate it with hornaments.

Why didn't the Christmas tree perform well on its algebra test?

It got stumped by the questions.

Why wouldn't Ebenezer Scrooge eat at the pasta restaurant?

It cost a pretty penne.

What do you call a cat who works for Santa?

Santa Claws.

How does a Christmas tree keep its breath fresh?

Orna-mints.

What do you call an old snowman?

A puddle.

Why does Santa go down the chimney on Christmas Eve?

It soots him.

What do you call Rudolph with tinsel in his ears?

Anything you want – he can't hear you.

Who tells the best Christmas jokes?

Reindeer. They sleigh every time.

Where do you find reindeer?

It depends on where you leave them.

Why is the turkey never hungry at Christmas?

It's stuffed.

What does Santa use to bake cakes?

Elf-raising flour.

Why has Santa been banned from sooty chimneys?

Carbon footprints.

What do you get if you put a bell on a skunk?

Jingle smells.

What falls at the North Pole but never gets hurt?

Snow.

What do you call an elf who just won the lottery?

Welfy.

How did the ornament get addicted to Christmas?

He was hooked on trees his whole life.

What's the difference between a reindeer and a knight?

One slays a dragon, the other drags a sleigh.

What did the farmer get for Christmas?

A cowculator.

What do you get if Santa forgets to wear his underwear?

St Nickerless.

What do the elves call it when Santa claps his hands at the end of a play?

Santapplause.

Which Christmas carol do dogs like best?

'Bark the Herald Angels Sing'

How can you keep your home warm at Christmas?

Tinsulation.

Why is Santa so chill?

He likes to live in the present, man.

Who is Rudolph's favourite pop star?

Beyon-sleigh.

Why did no one bid for Rudolph and Blitzen on eBay?

Because they were two deer.

What do you call an elf that can sing and dance?

Elfis.

HALLOWEEN HOWLS

What room does a ghost not need?

A living room.

What is a monster's favourite dessert?

I scream.

What kind of music do mummies love?

Wrap music.

Why didn't the skeleton go to school?

His heart wasn't in it.

What kind of dog does Dracula have?

A bloodhound.

What is a ghost's nose full of?

Boo-gers.

Why did the zombie skip school?

He was feeling rotten.

What instrument does a skeleton play?

The trom-bone.

How do ghosts wash their hair?

With sham-boo.

What is a witch's favourite subject in school?

Spelling.

Which monster plays the best tricks on Halloween?

Prank-enstein.

What do you call a witch who goes to the beach?

A sand-witch.

Why didn't the skeleton go to the dance?

He had no body to go with.

What do you get when you cross a snowman with a vampire?

Frostbite.

Why are ghosts the worst liars?

You can see right through them.

What did the pumpkin say to its carver?

'Cut it out!'

How do you know when a ghost is sad?

He starts boo-hooing.

Who did the zombie take to the party?

His ghoul-friend.

What kind of horse does a ghost ride?

A night-mare.

How do mummies tell their future?

They read their horror-scope.

Why did the vampire read the newspaper?

He heard it had great circulation.

What's the problem with twin witches?

You never know which witch is which.

How do you know you've been ghosted?

The poltergeist doesn't text you back.

How do vampires get around on Halloween?

On blood vessels.

Which streets do ghosts haunt?

Dead ends.

What's it like to be kissed by a vampire?

It's a pain in the neck.

Why don't zombies eat popcorn with their hands?

They eat their hands separately.

What do you call two witches who live together?

Broom-mates.

Where does a mummy go on holiday?

The Dead Sea.

Why did Dracula take cold medicine?

He was coffin too much.

What do you call a movie about zombies finding true love?

A zom-com.

Why are skeletons so calm?

Nothing gets under their skin.

Why did the headless horseman go into business?

He wanted to get ahead in life.

Why didn't the skeleton go to the scary movie?

He didn't have the guts.

Why did the ghost starch his sheet?

He wanted to scare everyone stiff.

What is a skeleton's favourite song?

'Bad to the Bone'

Why did the skeleton start a fight?

He had a bone to pick.

What kind of medicine do witches use on their warts?

I don't know, but it's not working.

What's a pumpkin's favourite genre?

Pulp fiction.

What kind of weather does a zombie like best?

Cloudy with a chance of brain.

What do you call a skeleton who goes out in the snow?

A numb-skull.

What's a zombie's favourite treat?

Eye candy.

Why are vampires easily fooled?

They're suckers.

Why don't werewolves ever know the time?

They're not whenwolves.

Do you know any skeleton jokes?

Yes, but you wouldn't find them very humerus.

Why aren't zombies ever arrested?

They can't be captured alive.

Did you hear about the coffin sale?

That's the last thing I need.

Why are vampires bad at art?

They're only able to draw blood.

I scream, you scream,
we all scream for
ice cream!

Silly Sally swiftly shooed
seven silly sheep.
The seven silly sheep
Silly Sally shooed
Shilly-shallied south.
These sheep shouldn't
sleep in a shack;
Sheep should sleep in a shed.

EASTER-ICAL

Why was the Easter Bunny so upset?

It was having a bad hare day.

What is a rabbit's favourite dance?

The Bunny Hop.

Why shouldn't you tell an Easter egg a good joke?

It might crack up.

What do you call a rabbit who tells jokes?

A funny bunny.

What happened when the Easter Bunny met the rabbit of its dreams?

They lived hoppily ever after.

How many chocolate bunnies can you put into an empty Easter basket?

Only one because after that, it's not empty.

What do you call a rabbit with fleas?

Bugs Bunny.

Why did the Easter egg hide?

He was a little chicken.

What day does an Easter egg hate the most?

Fry-day.

Why doesn't the Easter Bunny get hot?

It has hare conditioning.

What does the Easter Bunny say after it burps?

Eggs-cuse me.

Why don't you see dinosaurs at Easter?

They are eggs-tinct.

What do you call the funniest guest at Easter dinner?

The Easter ham.

Where does the Easter Bunny get its eggs?

From an egg plant.

What do you call an Easter egg from outer space?

An egg-stra-terrestrial.

What do you get if you pour boiling water down a rabbit hole?

Hot cross bunnies.

How can you tell where the Easter Bunny has been?

Eggs mark the spot.

Why did the Easter Bunny cross the road?

No bunny knows.

Why is Easter breakfast so fun?

Everyone cracks yolks.

How does an Easter chick dress for Sunday?

Im-peck-ably.

Where does Christmas come before Easter?

The dictionary.

How can you make Easter preparations go faster?

Use the eggs-press lane.

What kind of jewellery is the best Easter gift?

A 14-carrot gold necklace.

How does the Easter bunny leave?

It makes an eggs-it.

Why is the Easter Bunny such a good listener?

It's all ears.

Why did the Easter Bunny fail?

It put all its eggs in one basket.

What did the Easter Bunny say to the carrot?

'Nice gnawing you.'

How does the Easter Bunny keep its fur looking good?

Hare spray.

How does the Easter Bunny travel?

By hare-plane.

What happened when the Easter Bunny got kicked out of school?

It was egg-spelled.

What do you call a mischievous egg?

A practical yolk-er.

Did you hear about the bunny that sat on a bumblebee?

It's a tender tail.

What do Easter chicks have to do before they can become hens?

Pass their eggs-ams.

Why do you need a licence to hunt for Easter eggs?

No poaching is allowed.

What do you call a very tired Easter egg?

Eggs-austed.

What is the Easter Bunny's favourite sport?

Basket-ball.

Why did the Easter Bunny cross the road?

He saw the chicken doing it and thought it looked egg-citing.

What do you call a forgetful rabbit?

Hare-brained.

Why did the bunnies go on strike?

They wanted a better celery.

Why couldn't the rabbit fly home for Easter?

He couldn't afford the hare fare.

What do you get if you cross a frog with a rabbit?

A bunny ribbit.

Where do rabbits go after their wedding?

On their bunnymoon.

Where does Dracula keep his Easter candy?

In his Easter casket.

How does the Easter bunny stay in shape?

Lots of eggs-ercise.

How can you tell which rabbits are getting old?

Look for the gray hares.

How do you know a rabbit is in a good mood?

He's hoppy.

What did the magician say after the rabbit vanished?

Hare today, gone tomorrow.

What do you call a transformer bunny?

Hop-timus Prime.

How does a rabbit throw a tantrum?

He gets hopping mad.

Why did the rabbit bring toilet paper to the party?

He was a party pooper.

What do you call a zen egg?

An ommmmmmlet.

Why did the Easter Bunny have to fire the duck?

He kept quacking the eggs.

Why is the Easter Bunny so lucky?

He has four rabbits' feet.

What do you call a rabbit with the sniffles?

A runny bunny.

KNOCK, KNOCK

(PLEASE DON'T)

Knock, knock.
Who's there?
Boo.
Boo who?
Aww, don't cry.

Knock, knock.
Who's there?
Weekend.
Weekend who?
Weekend do anything we want.

Knock, knock.
Who's there?
Kanga.
Kanga who?
I believe it's pronounced kangaroo.

Knock, knock.
Who's there?
Chickens.
Chickens who?
Owls hoo. Chickens cluck.

Knock, knock.
Who's there?
Beets.
Beets who?
Beets me.

Knock, knock.
Who's there?
Spell.
Spell who?
W-H-O.

Knock, knock.
Who's there?
Howard.
Howard who?
Howard I know?

Knock, knock.
Who's there?
Butter.
Butter who?
Butter open the door. It's hot out here and I'm melting.

Knock, knock.
Who's there?
Etch.
Etch who?
Bless you.

Knock, knock.
Who's there?
Lettuce.
Lettuce who?
Lettuce in.

Knock, knock.
Who's there?
Wooden shoe.
Wooden shoe who?
Wooden shoe like to hear another joke?

Knock, knock.
Who's there?
Interrupting cow.
Interrupting c–
MOO!

Knock, knock.
Who's there?
Candice.
Candice who?
Candice joke get any worse.

Knock, knock.
Who's there?
Mikey.
Mikey who?
Mikey doesn't fit the keyhole.

Knock, knock.
Who's there?
Tank.
Tank who?
You're welcome.

Knock, knock.

Who's there?

Ice cream.

Ice cream who?

Ice cream if you don't let me in.

Knock, knock.

Who's there?

Luke.

Luke who?

Luke through the keyhole and you'll see.

Knock, knock.

Who's there?

You.

You who?

You who, anybody home?

Knock, knock.
Who's there?
Goliath.
Goliath who?
Goliath down, you look-eth tired.

Knock, knock.
Who's there?
Broccoli.
Broccoli who?
Broccoli doesn't have a last name.

Knock, knock.
Who's there?
A little old lady.
A little old lady who?
I didn't know you could yodel.

Knock, knock.
Who's there?
A herd.
A herd who?
A herd you were home, so I came straight over.

Knock, knock.
Who's there?
Frank.
Frank who?
Frank you for being my friend.

Knock, knock.
Who's there?
Dishes.
Dishes who?
Dishes the police – open the door.

Knock, knock.
Who's there?
Figs.
Figs who?
Figs the doorbell - I've been knocking for ages.

Knock, knock.
Who's there?
Cash.
Cash who?
No thanks, but I'll take a peanut if you have one.

Knock, knock.
Who's there?
Canoe.
Canoe who?
Canoe come out to play?

Knock, knock.
Who's there?
Stopwatch.
Stopwatch who?
Stopwatch you're doing and let me in.

Knock, knock.
Who's there?
Justin.
Justin who?
Justin the neighbourhood and thought I'd pop in.

Knock, knock.
Who's there?

One-One was a racehorse.
Two-Two was one, too.
When One-One won one race,
Two-Two won one, too.

I wish to wish the wish
you wish to wish,
but if you wish the
wish the witch wishes,
I won't wish the wish
you wish to wish.

THESE JOKES STINK!

Wanna hear a poop joke?

Nah, they always stink.

Why did the toilet paper roll down the hill?

To get to the bottom.

What did one toilet say to the other?

'You look flushed.'

What does a cloud wear under its raincoat?

Thunderwear.

Why can't you hear a pterodactyl go to the bathroom?

Because the pee is silent.

What do you call a teacher who refuses to fart in public?

A private tutor.

What did the poo say to the fart?

'You blow me away.'

Who are the most dangerous farters in the world?

Ninjas. They're silent but deadly.

Did you fart?

No, that was my butt blowing you a kiss.

Why did the baker have smelly hands?

He kneaded a poo.

What's invisible and smells like worms?

A bird fart.

What do you get when a duchess farts?

A noble gas.

Why did the fart miss graduation?

It got expelled.

Why did the cop sit on the toilet?

To do his duty.

What did one butt cheek say to the other?

'Together, we can stop this crap.'

Why didn't the toilet paper make it across the street?

It got stuck in a crack.

Why did Tigger stick his head in the toilet?

To look for Pooh.

How do you help a constipated person?

You scare the poop out of them.

What did one fly say to the other?

'Is this stool taken?'

What do you find inside a clean nose?

Fingerprints.

Did you hear about the film *Constipated*?

It never came out.

What do you call a vegetarian with diarrhoea?

Salad shooter.

Why was the sand wet?

The sea weed.

What did Sheriff Pee say to the bank robber?

'Urine trouble.'

My father, my grandfather and my great-grandfather all have diarrhoea.

It runs in my family's jeans.

Once upon a time, bottoms ruled the world.

It was a pants time.

How do you stop your nose from running?

Take away its shoes.

There are two reasons you shouldn't drink from the toilet.

Number one and number two.

How do you make a tissue dance?

Put a little boogie in it.

Why does your nose get tired in winter?

It runs all day.

How do a clown's farts smell?

Funny.

What do you call a skinny booger?

Slim pickings.

Did you pick your nose?

No, I was born with it.

What's big, brown and behind the wall?

Humpty's dump.

What do you call a documentary on boogers and snot?

Engrossing.

What's another name for a snail?

A booger wearing a crash helmet.

What did the booger say to the finger?

'Pick on someone your own size.'

What did the booger write in its Valentine's Day card?

'I'd pick you first.'

People keep asking me if I helped elect the booger.

I keep telling them he wasn't my pick.

What's the difference between boogers and broccoli?

Kids don't eat broccoli.

What does a booger tell its true love?

'I'm stuck on you.'

What comes out of your nose at 150 kilometres per hour?

A Lambogreeny.

The great Greek grape growers grow great Greek grapes.

Betty Botter bought a bit of butter but the bit of butter was too bitter, so Betty bought a better bit of butter to make the bitter butter better.

CRIMINALLY
BAD JOKES

Why did the robber jump in the shower?

He wanted to make a clean getaway.

What did the duck detective say to his partner?

'Let's quack this case.'

What do you call an empty bank?

A crime scene.

What did the policeman say to his tummy?

'Freeze! You're under a vest.'

Why do detectives have such bad posture?

They always have a hunch.

What kind of shoes do robbers wear?

Sneakers.

What's a good name for a detective?

Mr E.

What do you call someone who sees a crime at an Apple store?

An iWitness.

Why do potatoes make good detectives?

They always have their eyes peeled.

Why did the police detective suspect the artist?

He was sketchy.

Where do pirate detectives work?

Scotland Yarrrrrrd.

Why did the coffee go to the police?

It got mugged.

What happened when thieves stole a toilet?

The police had nothing to go on.

Why did the police go to the baseball game?

They heard someone was stealing a base.

What happens when a police officer goes to bed?

He becomes an undercover cop.

Why did the thief wear blue gloves?

He didn't want to be caught red-handed.

Why did the police arrest a bottle of water?

It was wanted in three different states: solid, liquid and gas.

What did the criminal say when police charged him with assaulting a man with a sheet of sandpaper?

'I just roughed him up a bit.'

Who is the world's most famous lawn detective?

Sherlock Gnomes.

Who works in tandem with the grammar police?

Corrections officers.

Did you hear about the criminal who stole a lamp?

He got a very light sentence.

What did police detectives say when they found a knife and a clock at a crime scene?

'Someone's been killing time.'

Want to hear a crime scene joke?

Well, move along, there's nothing to see here.

What do you call a crocodile who investigates crimes?

An investi-gator.

Why did the credit card go to jail?

It was guilty as charged.

Why couldn't the police solve the murder at a construction site?

The evidence wasn't concrete.

What's the difference between a good lawyer and a great lawyer?

A good lawyer knows the law.
A great lawyer knows the judge.

Why did the picture go to jail?

It was framed.

What do you call a detective electrician?

Sherlock Ohms.

Why did the judge send the turtle to jail?

He was known as a hard case.

Six slimey snails slid slowly seaward.

Whether the weather be fine or whether the weather be not, whether the weather be cold or whether the weather be hot, we'll weather the weather whatever the weather, whether we like it or not.

A-MOO-SING

ANIMAL JOKES

Why couldn't the pony sing a lullaby?

She was a little horse.

What do you call a dog magician?

A labracadabrador.

How do you get a squirrel to like you?

Act like a nut.

What did the Dalmatian say after lunch?

'That hit the spot.'

How do you make an octopus laugh?

With ten-tickles.

Why do ducks have feathers?

To cover their butt quacks.

What do you call a sleeping bull?

A bull-dozer.

What did the farmer call the cow that had no milk?

An udder failure.

Why do fish live in salt water?

Pepper makes them sneeze.

What do you get from a pampered cow?

Spoiled milk.

What sound do porcupines make when they kiss?

Ouch!

What kind of lion never roars?

A dandelion.

What is a cat's favourite colour?

Purrr-ple.

What do you give a sick pig?

Oinkment.

Why did the chewing gum cross the road?

It was stuck on the chicken's foot.

How do bears keep cool?

They use bear-conditioning.

Why are cats good at video games?

They have nine lives.

What has six legs and three eyes?

One and a half cats.

Where do baby apes sleep?

In apricots.

What did the crocodiles say when they turned up in the same outfit?

'Snap!'

What do you call a lazy kangaroo?

A pouch potato.

What did the duck say when he bought a new lipstick?

'Can you put it on my bill?'

What do you call the horse that lives next door?

The neighbour.

My dog is a genius. I asked him, 'What's two minus two?'

He said nothing.

What do you call a fish with no eyes?

A fssshh.

What is black and white and red all over?

A sunburnt zebra.

What do you call a bear with no teeth?

A gummy bear.

What do you call a fly without wings?

A walk.

Why did the chicken cross the road?

The KFC employee was chasing him.

What do you call a cow on a trampoline?

A milkshake.

Where do you find a dog with no legs?

Where you left him.

What do you call an elephant that doesn't matter?

An irrelephant.

What do you call a penguin in the Sahara desert?

Lost.

What do you call a pile of cats?

A meow-tain.

What animal can jump higher than a building?

Any animal – buildings don't jump.

What do you call a dishonest reptile?

A crookodile.

How does a penguin build its house?

Igloos it.

Every time I take my dog to the park, the ducks try to bite him.

That's what I get for buying a pure bread dog.

What do you call a cow with bad manners?

Beef jerky.

What do frogs wear on their feet?

Open toad sandals.

Where do sheep go on holiday?

The Baaaahamas.

What do you call a famous fish?

A starfish.

What goes 99-thump, 99-thump?

A centipede with a wooden leg.

What do you say to a rabbit on its birthday?

'Hoppy Birthday.'

Why do cows wear bells?

Their horns don't work.

Why do bees have sticky hair?

They use honeycombs.

What's black, white and blue?

A sad zebra.

What did the horse say when he walked into the bar?

Ouch.

If a dog chews shoes,
whose shoes does
he choose?

How much wood would a
woodchuck chuck if a woodchuck
could chuck wood?
He would chuck, he would,
as much as he could, and chuck
as much wood
as a woodchuck would if a
woodchuck could chuck wood.

SNORASAURUS DINO JOKES

What kind of dinosaur loves to sleep?

A stega-snore-us.

What do you call a dinosaur with an extensive vocabulary?

A thesaurus.

What did the T-Rex use to cut wood?

A dino-saw.

What makes more noise than a dinosaur?

Two dinosaurs.

What do you call a dinosaur that refuses to take a bath?

A stink-o-saurus.

What's the best way to talk to a dinosaur?

Long distance.

Why did carnivorous dinosaurs only eat raw meat?

They didn't know how to barbecue.

What do you get when a dinosaur walks through a strawberry patch?

Strawberry jam.

What is as big as a dinosaur but weighs nothing?

A dinosaur's shadow.

What do you call a dinosaur who wears glasses?

A do-you-think-he-saurus.

What does a triceratops sit on?

Its tricera-bottom.

What game does the brontosaurus like to play with humans?

Squash.

What dinosaur would Harry Potter be?

The Dinosorcerer.

How do you invite a dinosaur to a cafe?

'Tea, Rex?'

What do you call a dinosaur wearing a cowboy hat and boots?

Tyrannosaurus Tex.

Why did the archaeopteryx catch the worm?

It was an early bird.

What do you call a dinosaur that won't stop talking?

A dino-bore.

Where do dinosaurs go shopping?

The dino-store.

What do you get if you cross a dinosaur with a pig?

Jurassic pork.

What do you call twin dinosaurs?

Pair-odactyls.

What do you call a dinosaur with one eye?

Eye-saur.

What do you call a dinosaur who loves to tell jokes?

A laugh-o-saurus.

What do you call a baby dinosaur?

A Wee-Rex.

What do you get if you cross a T-Rex with explosives?

Dino-mite.

What do you call a dinosaur ghost?

A scare-o-dactyl.

Why did the T-Rex cross the road?

Chickens hadn't evolved yet.

What do you call a dinosaur who is a noisy sleeper?

A tyranno-snore-us

What's the best way to raise a baby dinosaur?

With a crane.

What comes after extinction?

Y-stinction.

What comes after Y-stinction?

Z-end.

The bottom of the butter bucket is the buttered bucket bottom.

How many yaks could a yak pack pack if a yak pack could pack yaks?

TOTALLY TASTELESS FOOD JOKES

What did Baby Corn say to Mama Corn?

'Where's Pop Corn?'

What does the Invisible Man drink at snack time?

Evaporated milk.

Did you hear about the cheese factory explosion in France?

All that was left was de brie.

What did the cupcake tell its frosting?

'I'd be muffin without you.'

What do you give a sick lemon?

Lemon-aid.

What do you call a fake noodle?

An im-pasta.

What kind of bean can't grow in a garden?

A jelly bean.

How does a cucumber become a pickle?

It goes through a jarring experience.

What's worse than finding a worm in your apple?

Finding half a worm.

How do you make a lemon drop?

Just let it fall.

What type of cheese is not yours?

Nacho cheese.

Two peanuts were walking down the street.

One was a salted.

What two things can you never eat for breakfast?

Lunch and dinner.

What kind of cheese is made backwards?

Edam.

Why did the banana go to the doctor?

It wasn't peeling well.

Why couldn't the sesame seed leave the casino?

It was on a roll.

What did one pickle say to the other after falling on the ground?

'Dill with it.'

Where do you learn to make a banana split?

At sundae school.

What did the grape say when the elephant stepped on him?

Nothing – he just let out a little wine.

Who is a dessert's favourite actor?

Robert Brownie Jr.

What did the hungry computer eat?

Chips – one byte at a time.

How can you tell if an elephant has been in your fridge?

You'll find footprints in the cheesecake.

Did you hear the joke about the peanut butter?

I'm not telling you – you might spread it.

Why did the melon jump into the lake?

It wanted to be a watermelon.

Why did the tomato blush?

It saw the salad dressing.

What do you call a group of strawberries playing guitar?

A jam session.

Why should you never tell a pizza joke?

They're all too cheesy.

What did one slice of bread say to the other before a fight?

'You're toast.'

Where do hamburgers go dancing?

At a meatball.

What fruit can you never cheer up?

A blueberry.

DON'T BE A BAD SPORT
(TELL BAD JOKES INSTEAD)

Why did the golfer wear two pairs of pants?

In case he got a hole in one.

Why can't Cinderella play netball?

She always runs away from the ball.

What is something you can serve but never eat?

A volleyball.

Why did the basketball player bring his suitcase to the game?

He travelled a lot.

What does a cricket player have in common with a magician?

They both do hat tricks.

What is the hardest part about skydiving?

The ground.

What do you call a pig who plays basketball?

A ball hog.

What is a golfer's favourite letter?

Tee.

Why did the ballerina quit?

It was tutu hard.

What did the baseball glove say to the ball?

'Catch ya later.'

What race is never run?

A swimming race.

How do cricket players find something online?

They googly it.

What animal is best at hitting a baseball?

A bat.

Why are basketball players messy eaters?

They're always dribbling.

Why did Tarzan spend so much time on the golf course?

He was perfecting his swing.

What is an insect's favourite sport?

Cricket.

Why did the boy swim the backstroke?

He had just eaten and didn't want to swim on a full stomach.

Which cricket player is a superhero?

The Batman.

Why is weightlifting a tough sport?

The bar is set very high.

Why did the AFL ball quit the team?

He got tired of being kicked around.

What position does a ghost play in soccer?

Ghoulie.

How do rugby players deal with their problems?

They tackle them head on.

Why did the chicken get sent off?

For persistent fowl play.

Why did the basketball player go to jail?

He shot the ball.

What do vampire footballers have at half-time?

Blood oranges.

When is a baseball player like a thief?

When he steals a base.

Why do basketball players love cookies and milk?

They can dunk them.

Why are hockey players good at making friends?

They're pretty quick at breaking the ice.

What did one tennis ball say to the other tennis ball?

'See you round.'

What do you call a really good game of badminton?

Radminton.

RIDICULOUS RIDDLES

I am harder to catch the faster you run. What am I?

Your breath.

Give me a drink, and I will die. Feed me, and I'll get bigger. What am I?

A fire.

I begin and end with E but I only have one letter. What am I?

An envelope.

I appear once in a minute, twice in a moment, but not once in a thousand years. What am I?

The letter M.

I have many rings but no fingers. What am I?

A telephone.

I go up but I never come back down. What am I?

Your age.

I go all around the world but I never leave the corner. What am I?

A stamp.

I'm always at breakfast, lunch and dinner, but you never get to eat me. What am I?

Cutlery.

If you drop me, I'm sure to crack, but if you smile at me, I'll smile back. What am I?

A mirror.

I have a face but I can't smile. What am I?

A clock.

You'll find me in Earth, Mercury, Jupiter and Mars, but not in Venus or Neptune. What am I?

The letter R.

I have cities but no houses. I have forests but no trees. I have water but no fish. What am I?

A map.

You can break me without even touching me. What am I?

A promise.

The more of me you take, the more you leave behind. What am I?

Your footsteps.

I'm bright orange with green on top and I sound like a parrot. What am I?

A carrot.

I can be cracked, played, told or made. What am I?

A joke.

Nobody empties me, but I never stay full for long. What am I?

The moon.

I'm easy to get into but hard to get out of. What am I?

Trouble.

I get wet as I dry. What am I?

A towel.

I'm tall when I'm young, and I'm short when I'm old. What am I?

A candle.

I have a head and a tail but no body. What am I?

A coin.

You can make me but never hold me or see me. What am I?

Noise.

I have a head but no eyes, nose or mouth. What am I?

A lettuce.

I'm red and small and have a heart of stone. What am I?

A cherry.

You have to break me in order to use me. What am I?

An egg.

You cut me, slice me, dice me, but you're the one who cries. What am I?

An onion.

I am a room with no doors or windows. What am I?

A mushroom.

I have four legs up, four legs down, am soft in the middle and hard all around. What am I?

A bed.

I'm a word with six letters, but if you take away one, 12 remain. What word am I?

Dozens.

I make songs but I never sing. What am I?

A musical note.

I thought a thought but the thought I thought, wasn't the thought you thought I thought.

Swan swam over the
sea, swim, swan, swim!
Swan swam back again
well swum, swan!

WHY DID YOU HAVE TO TELL THESE?!

Why did Mozart hate chickens?

Because they run around screaming, *Bach! Bach! Bach!*

Why did the cookie go to the hospital?

It felt crummy.

Why did the man put his money in the freezer?

He wanted cold, hard cash.

Why is a toothless dog like a tree?

It has more bark than bite.

Why do fluorescent lights hum?

Because they forget the words.

Why do birds fly south in the winter?

It's too far to walk.

Why are frogs so happy?

They just eat whatever bugs them.

Why did the emu cross the road?

To prove it wasn't a chicken.

Why did the computer go to the doctor?

It had a virus.

Why did the traffic light turn red?

It had to change in the middle of the street.

Why do bananas have to put on sunscreen before they go to the beach?

They might peel.

Why did the cow cross the road?

To get to the udder side.

Why did the chicken cross the road?

The chicken next to him farted.

Why did the skeleton go to the restaurant?

For spare ribs.

Why does everyone want to be friends with Mushroom?

He's a fungi.

Why did the lettuce go the gym?

It wanted to get shredded.

Why didn't the donkey cross the road?

He saw what happened to the zebra.

Why did the puppy sit near the fire?

He wanted to be a hot dog.

Why can't the strawberry cross the road?

It would cause a traffic jam.

Why don't they play poker in the jungle?

Too many cheetahs.

Why did the booger cross the road?

It was being picked on.

Why did the man catch his nose?

It was running.

Why don't snowmen like carrot cake?

It tastes like boogers.

Why did the computer break up with the internet?

There was no connection.

Why did the kid throw a stick of butter out the window?

To see a butter-fly.

Why didn't the teddy bear eat dessert?

He was stuffed.

Why can't you trust atoms?

They make up everything.

Why did the pony get sent to his room?

He wouldn't stop horsing around.

Why do dogs float in water?

They are good buoys.

Why do dragons sleep during the day?

So they can fight knights.

Why do seagulls live by the sea?

If they lived by the bay, they'd be bagels.

Why did the man get fired from the orange juice factory?

Lack of concentration.

Why can't a leopard hide?

He's always spotted.

Why did the clock go to the principal's office?

It was tocking too much.

Why did the tailor go to the doctor?

She had pins and needles.

Why did the boy throw the clock out the window?

He wanted to see time fly.

TOO ANNOYING FOR ANYWHERE ELSE

How do you get Pikachu on a bus?

You poke him on.

What kind of car does a toy drive?

A Toyota.

What do you call a boomerang that won't come back?

A stick.

What do you think of that new diner on the moon?

The food was good, but there wasn't much atmosphere.

Why can't Elsa from *Frozen* have a balloon?

She will let it go, let it go.

How does a scientist freshen her breath?

With experi-mints.

What building in your town has the most stories?

The public library.

What did one volcano say to the other?

'I lava you.'

What is a tornado's favourite game?

Twister.

What fruit do twins love?

Pears.

What kind of tree fits in your hand?

A palm tree.

What did the left eye say to the right eye?

'Between us, something smells.'

What did one plate say to the other plate?

'Dinner's on me.'

What is brown, hairy and wears sunglasses?

A coconut on holiday.

Why is six afraid of seven?

Because seven eight nine.

Why was the maths book sad?

It had too many problems.

Why does nobody talk to circles?

There's no point.

Why couldn't the bicycle stand up by itself?

It was two tired.

What do you call a funny mountain?

Hill-arious.

Why is the equals sign so humble?

It isn't greater than or less than anyone else.

Why did the orange lose the race?

It ran out of juice.

How do you throw a party in outer space?

You planet.

What happened to the girl who was crushed by a pile of books?

She only had her shelf to blame.

How do you stop an astronaut's baby crying?

You rocket.

What gives you the power to walk through a wall?

A door.

What was the first animal in space?

The cow that jumped over the moon.

What did the buffalo say every time his kid left the house?

Bi-son.

What happened when two antennas got married?

The ceremony wasn't great but the reception was beautiful.

What do you call a vegetarian uni student?

A uni-corn.

Why should you never read a book about glue?

You won't be able to put it down.

What should you do if you only know 25 letters of the alphabet?

Figure out y.

How do you talk to a giant?

Use big words.

What did one wall say to the other?

'I'll meet you at the corner.'

Where does the general keep his armies?

In his sleevies.

What has more letters than the alphabet?

The post office.

How does the ocean say hello?

It waves.

What do you call someone who is an expert in reading maps?

A legend.

When does a joke turn into a dad joke?

When it becomes apparent.

Who earns a living driving their customers away?

A taxi driver.

Which hand is better to write with?

Neither - it's better to write with a pen.

How many lips does a flower have?

Tu-lips.

Which days of the week are the strongest?

Saturday and Sunday - all the others are weekdays.

What do you get if you cross a duck with a firework?

A firequacker.

How did one tectonic plate apologise to the other?

'My fault.'

What has four wheels and flies?

A garbage truck.

What's red and smells like blue paint?

Red paint.

What time is it when the clock strikes 13?

Time to get a new clock.

What did the elevator say when it sneezed?

'I'm coming down with something.'

Did you hear about the guy who got hit by the same bike every single day?

It was a vicious cycle.

What lives in the middle of the sea?

The letter e.

What's a total rip-off?

Velcro.

How many Aussies does it take to fire up the barbecue?

Two. Easy.

I lost 25% of my roof last night . . . oof.

What did the girl say to her fingers?

'I'm counting on you.'

What do you call a can opener that doesn't work?

A can't opener.

Which month of the year has 28 days?

All of them.

If you drop a yellow hat in the Red Sea, what does it become?

Wet.

What kind of cup doesn't hold water?

A cupcake.

How many seconds are in a year?

Twelve – one in each month.

How many letters are there in the alphabet?

Eleven: three in 'the' and eight in 'alphabet'.

Ms Jones has four daughters. Each daughter has a brother. How many kids are there in total?

Five. Each daughter has the same brother.

If two's a company and three's a crowd, what are four and five?

Nine.

What can run but not walk?

A nose.

What did the zero say to the eight?

'Nice belt.'

What has a bottom at the top?

Legs.

Cats have four, bugs have four, but school has six. What are they?

Letters.

Tom's parents have three kids. Their names are Huey, Dewey and ______?

Tom.

What did Jay-Z call his wife before they were married?

Feyoncé.

What has thousands of needles but cannot sew?

A porcupine.

Which question can you never answer 'yes' to?

'Are you asleep?'

What bird is always out of breath?

A puffin.

What do you get when you cross a centipede with a parrot?

A walkie talkie.

If practice makes perfect and perfect needs practice, I'm perfectly practiced and practically perfect.

A skunk sat on a stump
and thunk the stump
stunk, but the stump
thunk the skunk stunk.

PENGUIN BOOKS

UK | USA | Canada | Ireland | Australia
India | New Zealand | South Africa | China

Penguin Random House Australia is part of the Penguin Random House group of companies whose addresses can be found at global.penguinrandomhouse.com.

First published by Penguin Books, an imprint of Penguin Random House Australia Pty Ltd, in 2023

Cover and internal design and illustrations by Rebecca King © Penguin Random House Australia Pty Ltd

Internal icons: All background icons on pages 158–167 © balabolka/Shutterstock.com, all remaining background icons © Tiwat K/Shutterstock.com; Tongue Twister speech bubbles © nubenamo/Shutterstock.com.

Printed and bound in Australia by Griffin Press, an accredited ISO AS/NZS 14001 Environmental Management Systems printer

NATIONAL LIBRARY OF AUSTRALIA
A catalogue record for this book is available from the National Library of Australia

FSC www.fsc.org MIX Paper | Supporting responsible forestry FSC® C018684

ISBN 978 1 76 134619 4 (Paperback)

Penguin Random House Australia uses papers that are natural and recyclable products, made from wood grown in sustainable forests. The logging and manufacture processes are expected to conform to the environmental regulations of the country of origin.

penguin.com.au

We at Penguin Random House Australia acknowledge that Aboriginal and Torres Strait Islander peoples are the Traditional Custodians and the first storytellers of the lands on which we live and work. We honour Aboriginal and Torres Strait Islander peoples' continuous connection to Country, waters, skies and communities. We celebrate Aboriginal and Torres Strait Islander stories, traditions and living cultures; and we pay our respects to Elders past and present.